T865600010209N

940.53
LEV

Levy, Patricia.

Causes

$19.99

DATE DUE	BORROWER'S NAME	ROOM NO.
4-30	Julia Hoover	Mb
4-22-09	" "	
3-8-11	Landon Garrow	McCoy

T865600010209N

940.53
LEV

Levy, Patricia.

Causes

SO. BELOIT HIGH SCHOOL LIBRARY
SO. BELOIT, ILLINOIS

THE HOLOCAUST
CAUSES

Pat Levy

**RAINTREE
STECK-VAUGHN
PUBLISHERS**

A Harcourt Company

Austin   New York
www.raintreesteckvaughn.com

Published by Raintree Steck-Vaughn Publishers, an imprint of Steck-Vaughn Company

Library of Congress Cataloging-in-Publication Data
Levy, Patricia, 1951-
    The Holocaust causes / Pat Levy.
       p. cm.
    Includes bibliographical references (p.)and index.
    ISBN 0-7398-3257-3
      1. Holocaust, Jewish (1939–1945)--Causes--Juvenile literature.
    [1. Holocaust, Jewish (1939–1945)] I. Title.

    D804.34 .L49   2001
    940.53'18—dc21   00-055248

Printed in Italy. Bound in the United States.
1 2 3 4 5 6 7 8 9 0 05 04 03 02 01

Cover photos: The perimeter fence at Auschwitz concentration camp in Poland; Hitler in 1934 at the Bückeberg party rally.

Page 1: Jacqui on the Street by Felix Nussbaum. The artist and his wife were sent to Auschwitz in the last wave of Jewish deportations from Belgium. Both are believed to have perished in Auschwitz in 1944.

Acknowledgments

The author and publishers thank the following for their permission to reproduce photographs: AKG London: pages 1, 4, 5, 6b, 7, 13, 16, 17, 20, 21, 23, 30, 31 (top), 32, 34 (top), 36, 44, 45, 46, 47, 50, 56; Camera Press: cover (background photo), pages 52, 57; Hulton-Getty Picture Collection: pages 10, 18, 19 (bottom), 40; Imperial War Museum: pages 14, 24, 25, 31 (bottom), 49; Mary Evans Picture Library: cover (main photo), pages 8, 11, 12, 15 (top and bottom), 19 (top), 26, Popperfoto: pages 6 (top), 22 (top and bottom), 29, 33, 34 (bottom), 35, 37 (bottom), 38, 41, 42, 43, 54, 55, 58, 59; Topham Picturepoint: pages 37 (top), 48, 53; Wiener Library: page 27 (left and right).

CONTENTS

WHAT WAS THE HOLOCAUST?

LESS THAN 60 years ago, during World War II, the government of a civilized modern European country— Germany— deliberately murdered six million people because they were Jewish. This horror is known as the Holocaust. The murderous intentions of Germany's governing party at the time—the Nazis—also focused on others besides Jews. Ordinary German doctors and nurses killed 90,000 mentally or physically disabled people; 500,000 Gypsies were killed in concentration camps; and millions more were killed because they were homosexuals, communists, opponents of the Nazi regime, Poles, or Russians. It is estimated that more than five million other civilians died at the hands of the Nazis.

After the war, very few Holocaust survivors felt able to talk about their experiences. When they did, few people were interested. For the most part, it was not until the 1950s that people started to analyze what had happened and the term "Holocaust" began to be used by Jewish historians. In this book "the Holocaust" refers to this deliberate murder of millions of

Below: Jewish women workers in a special factory at the Auschwitz death camp collected and sorted the shoes of those who were gassed. This photo shows a small number of the shoes that were found when Auschwitz was liberated.

Jews and other minorities between 1941 and 1945.
Germany's regime, led by Adolf Hitler, called their policies "the
final solution to the Jewish question."

When Nazi Germany invaded the Soviet Union in June 1941,
millions of Jews in the Baltic states (Lithuania, Latvia, and
Estonia) and the Ukraine were executed by special units, known
as *Einsatzgruppen*. In addition, many thousands of Jews died of
cold and starvation in the ghettos set up by the Nazis in Polish
cities. Between 1941 and 1945 the Nazis established a
systematic plan to murder all the Jews in the European
territories they occupied. Six special extermination camps were
created for this purpose in Poland. There, Jews were killed in
large groups in gas chambers and their bodies burned in
crematoriums. Hundreds of thousands more died in the death
and concentration camps of disease, starvation, and overwork.

Above: Gypsies in confinement at the Belzec death camp in Poland. Gypsies were targeted by the Nazis because the Nazis believed them to be "work-shy" and "asocial."

Perpetrators and Bystanders

It would have been impossible to transport millions of victims from every Nazi-occupied country in Europe to the death camps of Poland without the active cooperation of thousands of people. Many historians discuss the genocide (destruction) of the European Jews as if it were carried out by only a relatively small group of soldiers. But ordinary German policemen rounded up the Jews, railroad workers assisted as they were put onto train cars, clerks in offices organized train timetables, and workers in fields watched as the cattle trains went past. Government officials administered and oversaw the massive program of extermination.

The first massacres in the Baltic states, the Ukraine, and Belorussia, were carried out by the *Einsatzgruppen*. However, many of the local people—Ukrainians, Lithuanians, and Latvians—assisted or took part. The *Einsatzgruppen* probably killed almost as many Jews as later died in the gas chambers.

The labor of prisoners in 1,600 labor camps and ghettos benefitted companies such as Daimler, an automobile manufacturer, or I.G. Farben, a huge chemical company.

Above: In the camps, German criminals were often chosen to oversee the slave labor of Jewish prisoners.

Below: Polish Jews are forced onto a freight train that is about to leave the station at Lodz.

Each of the major camps were staffed by about 5,000 Germans.

Although many Germans were bystanders, some actively resisted the Nazi regime, and some tried to help save Jews. In recent years historians have debated the issue of to what degree German society supported and aided the Holocaust.

How Nazi Policy Changed

It is possible to chart the changing policies of the Nazis toward the Jews as the Nazis power and influence grew:

1920s: verbal attacks on Jews in Germany

Early 1930s: physical attacks on property and persons and a few unsanctioned but unpunished murders

1933–34: removal of German Jews from civil service, journalism, higher education, and the arts

1935: legal and administrative measures to isolate and impoverish German Jews

1935–39: confiscation of property and permitted emigration of Jews from Germany and later Austria

1939: all Jewish men between 14 and 60 required to do forced labor; deaths caused by work conditions and starvation

1939–40: forced deportations of Jews to Poland and creation of the ghettos; deaths due to random massacres, disease, and starvation

1941: first organized mass murders by shooting and in gas vans; building of gas chambers and crematoriums

1942: mass deportations from all over occupied Europe to the death camps

1944: death marches of all remaining Jews across Germany in the face of the advancing Soviet army

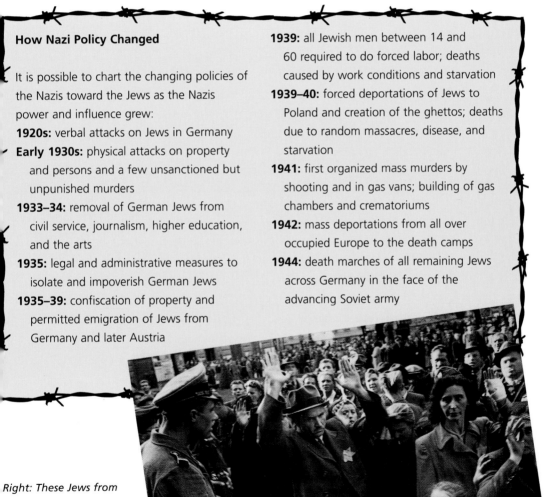

Right: These Jews from Budapest in Hungary were sent to the death camps in 1944, two or three months before the camps were abandoned.

WHY THE JEWS?

I N ORDER to understand how the Holocaust could take place, it may be helpful to look at the history of anti-Semitism in Europe. Anti-Semitism means hostility or discrimination toward Jews.

Judaism originated in what is now Israel, where the kingdom of Judah was established in modern-day Palestine in 922 B.C. In the 1st century B.C., Palestine came under Roman control when the last great Jewish rebellion was crushed by the Romans in 70 A.D., the Jewish diaspora began. Diaspora means the dispersal of the Jewish people from their ancient homelands in the Middle East.

The Jews settled throughout Europe and northern Africa. In most places, they were only partially accepted, set apart by religious and cultural differences and by Christian teachings that held them responsible for the death of Christ and thereby justified all manner of prejudice and discrimination against them.

Below: A medieval illustration of one kind of blood libel—the false belief that Jews murdered Christian babies to use their blood in the baking of bread.

The Middle Ages

The first massacres of Jews occurred in the 11th century, when French and English crusaders killed tens of thousands of German Jews. During the 12th century, myths about Jews sacrificing Christian children—the so-called blood libel—became widespread.

In 1215 the Pope decreed that Jews must wear a badge and distinctive clothing. Across Europe, Jews were restricted in their choice of occupation. In 1290 the Jews were expelled from England and in 1302 and 1332 from France. Because expulsion and discrimination often forced Jews to move from place to place, Jews were accused of spreading the plague, or Black Death, a disease that killed an estimated

one-third of Europe's population in the 14th century. By the end of the 15th century, Spain had expelled its large Jewish population.

Many Jews found refuge in Poland. For 300 years Jewish culture flourished in Poland, until 1648 when thousands of Jews were massacred or driven from their homes. Before the Holocaust, this represented the single greatest outbreak of organized anti-Jewish violence.

Below: Martin Luther, the 16th-century German Protestant thinker. Many Nazis used the teachings of Martin Luther to justify their own vicious anti-Semitism.

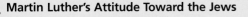

Martin Luther's Attitude Toward the Jews

Martin Luther was one of the architects of the Protestant Reformation, which arose out of a spirit of opposition to the corruption of the Catholic Church. At first, Jews hoped that Protestant reformers would be more tolerant than Catholics had been. But Luther himself was a vicious anti-Semite who wrote in 1543:

What then shall we Christians do with this damned rejected race of Jews?...we cannot tolerate them if we do not wish to share in their lies, curses, and blasphemy...Let me give you my honest advice.

First their synagogues ... should be set on fire, and whatever does not burn should be covered or spread over with dirt so that no one may ever be able to see a cinder or stone of it. Secondly, their homes should be likewise broken down and destroyed....Thirdly, they should be deprived of their prayer books and Talmuds in which their idolatry, lies, cursing, and blasphemy are taught. Fourthly, their rabbis must be forbidden under threat of death to teach any more....All their cash and valuables ought to be taken from them and put aside for safekeeping...everything that they possess they stole and robbed from us through their usury.

(Quoted in Martin Gilbert, *The Holocaust*)

The 19th Century

Throughout the 18th century, the ideas of the Enlightenment philosophers—a belief in freedom, democracy, and scientific logic—spread throughout Europe. As a result, in the early 19th century Jews throughout Western and Central Europe received emancipation, meaning they were granted many of the same rights as other members of society. Many Jews achieved success in commerce, politics, medicine, science, and the arts, particularly in the German states and the Austro-Hungarian Empire.

However, this new prominence led to resentment and renewed anti-Semitism. Jews were now blamed and feared as an economic threat. Many believed Jews could never be "true" or loyal citizens of the countries where they lived.

Most European Jews at this time lived on the western borders of Czarist Russia (which included Poland). When Czar Alexander II was assassinated in 1881, a new wave of pogroms (attacks on Jews)

Below: The German-Swiss physicist Albert Einstein (1879–1955), left, and the Austrian psychiatrist Sigmund Freud (1865–1939), right, pose with U.S. president Warren G. Harding, center. Einstein and Freud were both European Jews whose scientific achievements revolutionized modern society.

and expulsions began. This drove many Jews westward into the Austro-Hungarian and German empires and paved the way for the rise of Zionism, a political movement dedicated to the creation of a Jewish homeland or national state, preferably in Palestine. Two million Jews left Russia for the United States.

In the 1890s the Jews still thought of Germany as a haven, unaware that a new anti-Semitism was gaining strength there. In a depressed economy Jewish bankers and businessmen were blamed for closures, bankruptcies, and repossessions. People viewed them as both exploitive capitalists and disloyal communists, and several anti-Semitic political parties sprang up. These parties were supported by several prominent Germans, including the famous composer Richard Wagner, who was a friend of the king of Bavaria, Ludwig II.

Above: Friedrich Nietzsche (1844–1900) suggested the idea of a "master race."

Wagner was influenced by the philosopher Friedrich Nietzsche, who put forward the idea of the *Übermensch* (Superman)—a race of people who, because of their superior qualities, could impose their will on the weak and the worthless. Many anti-Semites, and later the Nazis, saw themselves as members of this "super race" and believed they were justified in going to any lengths to preserve its purity. In fact Nietzsche regarded anti-Semitism as wrong, but his ideas were distorted by anti-Semites and used for their own ends.

Richard Wagner on the Jews

In a letter to King Ludwig II, Wagner wrote: *I must certainly regard the Jewish race as the born enemy of pure man and of all nobility in them and am convinced that we Germans in particular will be destroyed by them.*

(Quoted in Ronnie W. Landau, *The Nazi Holocaust*)

Right: A contemporary cartoon of Richard Wagner (1813–1883)

By the second half of the 19th century, many Germans believed that Jews had to be removed from German society in order for it to thrive and prosper. In 1881 the economist Eugen Dühring claimed that Jews were "scarcely human" and were the enemies of all nations. In 1887 the German philosopher Paul de Lagarde described the Jews as "vermin" and called for a "surgical incision… to remove the source of the infection." Two years later, Houston Stewart Chamberlain published his bestselling book *Foundations of the Nineteenth Century*, which argued that the Jews were an evil race, determined to dominate the world. Chamberlain, the son-in-law of Wagner, claimed that there was a war between Germans and Jews and that this war was the most important struggle in world history. Politicians and newspaper editors began to describe the Jews as enemies of the German people.

The term "anti-Semitism" was first coined in 1879 by a German journalist, Wilhelm Marr, who founded the League of Anti-Semites. In the elections of 1898 anti-Semitic parties attracted about 4 percent of the total vote. By 1907, they had 16 deputies in the Reichstag (German parliament).

By the end of the 19th century, Jews had been driven across Europe several times, massacred by the thousands, and restricted in their choice of occupation and where to live. They had also been blamed for the death of Christ, accused of sacrificing Christian children, and of conspiring to undermine Christian life. All these accusations would eventually aid the Nazis in their program of elimination.

Right: Ernst Bassermann was the leader of the National Liberal party in the last decades of the 19th century.

The Protocols of the Elders of Zion

Near the end of the 19th century, the secret police in Russia forged a document to discredit Russia's Jews, many of whom were active opponents of the government. The document was alleged to have been written by Jewish leaders as part of a worldwide conspiracy to rule the world:

Whether the state is exhausted by internal convulsions or whether civil wars deliver it into the hands of external enemies, in either case it can be regarded as hopelessly lost: it is in our power....Only power can control in politics especially if it is concealed in talents which are necessary to statesmen. Violence must be the principle; hypocrisy and cunning the rule of those governments which do not wish to lay down their crowns at the feet of the agents of some new power. This evil is the sole means of attaining the good. For this reason we must not hesitate at bribery, fraud, and treason....

(Quoted in Paul Massing, *Rehearsal for Destruction*)

WORLD WAR I AND ITS AFTERMATH

B ETWEEN 1914 and 1918 Europe experienced mass death in war, a communist revolution in Russia, and huge political upheavals. For many people, Germans in particular, it seemed as if all the certainties of their lives were being overturned.

Germany's War

When World War I began in 1914, Germany had existed as a unified state for only fortysome years. It was ruled by Kaiser Wilhelm II and a cabinet. Its parliament was democratically elected but had little power. For a time liberal democratic politics had dominated the new state, but Germany, like much of Europe, was undergoing enormous social and political changes. Industrialization was forcing new practices on an old economic system. The middle classes, especially, blamed the Jews and socialism for all their country's problems.

Most Germans viewed World War I as a patriotic crusade that would allow Germany to take its place as the equal of the most powerful European states, Great Britain and France. The war was fought on two fronts. In the east, Germany defeated Russia

Below: Kaiser Wilhelm II inspects his troops in Riga, Latvia, in September 1917.

Left: From left to right, Marshal Ferdinand Foch of France; President Georges Clemenceau of France; Prime Minister David Lloyd George of Great Britain; Prime Minister Vittorio Orlando of Italy; and Foreign Minister Baron Sidney Sonnino of Italy at the Versailles negotiations.

by the end of 1917, but in the west, French, British, and U.S. troops eventually wore down the German forces. Demoralized by the impending defeat, Germans revolted in several major cities, forcing Kaiser Wilhelm to abdicate. The new German government soon agreed to peace terms.

The Treaty of Versailles

The peace treaty, signed at Versailles in France in June 1919, punished Germany severely. It lost 13 percent of its pre-war territory, along with six million subjects, all its colonies and overseas assets, large quantities of raw materials such as coal and iron, and much of its military. Germany was blamed for the war and made to pay $33 billion (compensation) in war reparations to Great Britain, Italy, and France.

Below: A German cartoon from the time shows Greed, Revenge, and other grotesque figures gloating over the Versailles treaty.

Europe's Jews and World War I

For most Germans, defeat in World War I was a great shock. So were the economic troubles—first, runaway inflation, then severe depression—that plagued Germany through the 1920s and early 1930s. The "humiliation" of the Versailles treaty was another blow. As Adolf Hitler and the National Socialist party began their rise to power in the late 1920s, they blamed a familiar target for Germany's problems—Jews.

Anti-Semites succeeded in making Jews the scapegoat for Germany's problems even though German Jews had proved themselves as loyal during World War I as any other Germans.

Left: Industrialist and philosopher Walther Rathenau, a Jew, served as foreign minister in Germany's postwar democratic government. He was assassinated in 1922.

The Nazi Manifesto

In February 1920 the National Socialist German Workers party (later known as the Nazis, by mixing the letters from the German words "National" and "Sozialistische"), published its manifesto. There were 25 points, some of which are listed below:

1. We demand the uniting of all Germans within one Greater Germany, on the basis of the right to self-determination of nations.

2. We demand equal rights for the German people with respect to other nations, and the annulment of the Peace Treaty of Versailles.

3. We demand land and soil to feed our people and settle our excess population.

4. ...Only persons of German blood can be nationals, regardless of religious affiliation. No Jew therefore can be a German national...

8. Any further immigration of non-Germans is to be prevented. We demand that all non-Germans who entered Germany after... 1914 be forced to leave the Reich [state] without delay.

18. We demand ruthless battle against those who harm the common good by their activities....usurers, profiteers, etc. are to be punished by death without regard to religion or race.

(Quoted in Ronnie S. Landau, *Studying the Holocaust*)

More than 100,000 Jews served in the German military during World War I; more than 12,000 of those were killed. Following the war, however, thousands of Jewish refugees from the countries east of Germany—Poland, Ukraine, Belarus, the Baltic Nations—moved to Germany to escape civil war and oppression. With Germany's economy suffering, it was easy to target these refugees as one of the causes.

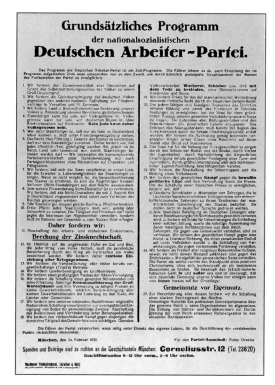

Right: A page from the Nazi Manifesto

Zionism and Palestine

Zionism, the belief that the Jews should have a homeland in Palestine, began to emerge in the 1890s. The movement gathered strength in 1894 when Alfred Dreyfus, a Jewish officer in the French army, was unjustly accused of selling military secrets to Germany. The case provoked a wave of anti-Semitism across France and confirmed the Zionists' belief that the Jews' only hope of security lay in a state of their own. In 1896 Theodor Herzl, an Austrian journalist, published his book *Jewish State*, which launched the Zionist movement.

The Zionists were effective in their efforts to persuade European governments to give their support to the proposed Jewish homeland in Palestine. By November 1917, it appeared likely that World War I would result in Britain gaining control of Palestine from the Ottoman Empire. That month, the British foreign secretary, Arthur Balfour, wrote Lord Lionel Rothschild, head of the Zionist movement in Britain, that the government of Great Britain supported the establishment of a Jewish homeland in Palestine.

Left: Lord Lionel Rothschild (1886–1937), was a leader of the Zionist movement in Great Britain.

Zionists were thrilled by the Balfour Declaration, but Great Britain's support was not as strong as they had hoped. Palestinian Arabs opposed the creation of a Jewish state, and after World War I, Great Britain needed Arab support.

Right: Arthur Balfour (1848–1930) was foreign secretary of Great Britain during World War I.

Below: British troops enter Jerusalem near the end of World War I.

German Reactions to Zionism

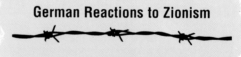

Nazi reactions to the Zionist movement were complex. On the one hand Nazis viewed German Zionist organizations as part of the international Jewish conspiracy. On the other hand they welcomed the idea of sending Germany's Jews somewhere else. In the 1930s, they made an agreement with Zionist organizations to exchange 60,000 German Jews for 100 million Reichsmarks worth of German goods. This was known as the Haavarah Agreement.

HITLER AND NAZISM

ADOLF HITLER was born in Austria in 1889. He had an unremarkable childhood in Linz, where he failed to graduate from high school and showed insufficient talent to get into art school.

After 1908 the 20-year-old Hitler lived in Vienna, on a tiny income from his family, and drifted. At this stage, wanting to find someone to blame for his failure, he began to formulate right-wing ideas and to talk about them to anyone who would listen. He was not untypical—many Viennese middle-class people held right-wing views and were anti-Semitic. In 1914 Hitler joined the German army; he was decorated several times during the war for bravery. After the war, while still in the military, he was asked to spy on several of the new political parties in Munich. One of these was a right-wing group, *Deutsche Arbeiterpartei*, (DAP). Impressed with their views, Hitler joined. He soon discovered a talent as a public speaker and became the party's leader. This group would become the Nazi party.

The Rise of the Far Right

Trying to steer a moderate, liberal course, Germany's postwar governments were thereby vulnerable to attack from both the political left and right. In Russia, communists had taken power and many Germans felt Germany should follow the same path. There were two attempted left-wing coups, both led by Jewish communists, in 1918 and 1919. In 1923 French and Belgian troops occupied the Ruhr, Germany's industrial heartland, over Germany's failure to pay war reparations. Economic collapse followed. Faced with huge debts, the government printed millions of banknotes that quickly became worthless as hyperinflation set in. When the currency lost all its value, thousands of businesses were forced to close and many individuals lost their life savings.

Above: Seen here in November 1914, Adolf Hitler served in the German army during World War I.

All this helps to explain the growing popularity of extreme right-wing groups who, rather than face the real causes of Germany's defeat and economic collapse, were eager to find a scapegoat. By 1921 Hitler had become the leader of the Nazi party, one of several right-wing groups that were becoming major forces in German politics.

By 1933, 400 anti-Semitic organizations were holding regular meetings and publishing 700 anti-Semitic periodicals. The more mainstream political parties began to shed Jewish representatives, and by 1930 the party most closely associated with Jewish issues, the Social Democrats, had lost all its Jewish members.

Left: In postwar Germany, inflation grew so bad that people had to carry their cash in a wheelbarrow when they went shopping. These children are playing with stacks of worthless banknotes.

A Brief Setback

By November 1923 Hitler felt he had enough support to mount his own coup d'état. He and his supporters tried to recruit followers in a beer hall, but the Beer Hall Putsch, as his attempt to overthrow the government became known, was easily put down. Hitler was arrested and sentenced to five years imprisonment for treason but served only nine months. He used his trial as an opportunity to accuse Jews of undermining the country and spent the time in jail writing his autobiographical attack on the Jews, *Mein Kampf* ("My Struggle").

Once Hitler came out of jail, the Nazis concentrated on legal ways of seeking power. In 1924, at the height of the economic crisis, the Nazi Party gained 6 percent of the national vote. They found that they could appeal to minority interests and began to form groups that would appeal to small blocs of voters for different reasons. The Hitler Youth and a students' association, for example, were developed with future voters in mind in 1926. These were followed by school students' unions, a jurists' association, a physicians' association, a teachers' association, and the League of Struggle for German Culture (aimed at those in the arts). All these organizations encouraged their members to push out

Above: Nazi stormtroopers, also known as Brownshirts, parade past the Brandenburg Gate. The stormtroopers were the "muscle" of the Nazi party.

Die Angeklagten des Hitler-Prozesses.

Pernet   Weber   Frick   Kriebel   Ludendorff   Hitler   Brückner   Wagner
Röhm

Left: Hitler with German military supporters of the Beer Hall Putsch.

Jewish colleagues. In addition Nazis became prominent members of a small-store owners' association whose aim was to put the largely Jewish-owned department stores out of business.

The 1929 crash of the New York stock market deepened the economic depression that had already begun to affect Germany. In this troubled climate, the Nazis' strategy of appealing to disaffected groups began to pay off. In 1930 they got 6.5 million votes (18 percent of the national vote), entitling them to 107 seats in the Reichstag. The 1932 election saw even greater numbers voting Nazi (37 percent of the electorate). Now a powerful national figure, Hitler refused to take part in government unless he was appointed to the position of chancellor—the head of the government.

How did Hitler become chancellor of Germany? The German constitution decreed that if the Reichstag ever became unable to function efficiently, the president could run the country on an emergency basis. After 1930, many small parties were represented in the Reichstag, but none had a majority. The biggest party was the Nazis, but they could not persuade enough of the smaller groups in the Reichstag to agree to form a governing coalition with them. Governing by emergency decree, President Paul von Hindenburg, a military hero of World War I, was eventually convinced to offer Hitler the chancellorship in January 1933.

Below: Chancellor Hitler greets President Hindenburg on March 21, 1933, at the opening of the new Reichstag.

Who Voted for Hitler and Why?

1. First-time voters and very young people who had joined the Hitler Youth Movement or one of the other groups aimed at young people.
2. Farmers, because the Nazi Party offered the hope of an end to the agricultural depression and because of long-standing rural anti-Semitism.
3. People who had been put out of business by the new mass production techniques (small craftsmen, small-store owners, other small businessmen, and low-level civil servants).
4. Many people who had previously been liberal voters but who had become exasperated by the endless disputes among the smaller, more moderate parties.
5. The upper classes, especially those living in areas where there were large numbers of wealthy Jews.
6. A large proportion of ordinary working people. Generally speaking, the working classes either voted Nazi or communist. Having endured so much poverty, most of them wanted a radical solution to Germany's problems.

Hitler's supporters clearly had very different needs and viewpoints and, under normal circumstances, it is difficult to imagine these groups having much in common. But these were not normal circumstances. Several historians now suggest that, in voting for the Nazis, many people were voting *against* Germany's postwar government rather than *for* any particular set of policies.

What Exactly Was Nazi Policy?

The Nazis sought to provide an explanation and a solution for Germany's problems. Their ideas had been popular for many years. Nazi ideology suggested that the strength of the German people lay in a sense of *Volksgemeinschaft*, or national community. According to the Nazis, German racial purity was the strength of the German nation. Germany's problems—including

Above: This Nazi propaganda poster from World War II bears the confident slogan "Victory is ours!"

losing the war and its economic collapse—resulted from the contamination of that purity by "inferior" peoples such as Jews.

The weakness of the young German democracy helped create the conditions in which the Nazis could flourish. Between 1928 and 1933, when Hitler became chancellor, the Nazis actually downplayed their anti-Semitism when appealing to certain parts of society. For much of the electorate, the stand the Nazis took against communism and trade unionism was probably the most attractive aspect of their policy.

Above: Another Nazi poster uses the image of a blonde, blue-eyed German girl. She encourages people to give money to "Build youth hostels and homes."

Middle-class Attitudes Towards Jews

Melita Maschmann, a member of the Hitler Youth Movement and the daughter of well-educated parents, remembers how she and her friends regarded the Jews:

As children we had been told fairy stories which sought to make us believe in witches and wizards. Now we were too grown-up to take this witchcraft seriously, but we still went on believing in the "wicked Jews." They had never appeared to us in bodily form, but it was our daily experience that adults believed in them. After all, we could not check to see if the earth was round rather than flat—or to be more precise, it was not a proposition we thought it necessary to check. The grown-ups "knew" it and one took over this knowledge without mistrust. They also "knew" that the Jews were wicked. The wickedness was directed against the prosperity, unity, and prestige of the German nation, which we had learned to love from an early age. The anti-Semitism of my parents was a part of their outlook which was taken for granted.

(Quoted in Daniel Goldhagen, *Hitler's Willing Executioners*)

Hitler's Political Views

In *Mein Kampf*, published in 1924, Hitler described a world where so-called Aryans—blond-haired northern Europeans—fought a never-ending battle with their arch-enemies, the Jews and the Slavs, who sought to destroy the purity of the race by defiling German women. Their ultimate goal, Hitler wrote, was world domination, by means of infiltrating political, economic, and social systems. According to Hitler, this was what had happened to Russia, when the Czar had been overthrown by "Jewish Bolsheviks." Hitler argued that just as evolution proceeded through the "survival of the fittest" animals, so, too, the various human races compete for survival.

Hitler believed that the only way for the German race to survive was to fight—against the Jews in their own country, and against other "inferior races" (Slavic peoples, such as the Russians and Poles) in order to expand their homeland. He frequently likened Jews to "filth" and "disease," and at one stage expressed his wish that more German Jewish soldiers had died in World War I: "If twelve or fifteen thousand of these Hebrew corrupters of the people had been held under poison gas, as happened to the hundreds of thousands of our very best German workers in the field, the sacrifice of millions at the front would not have been in vain."

Below: A popular English translation of Mein Kampf *from the 1930s*

Deutſche Jugend   Jüdiſche Jugend

14jähriger deutſcher Junge   14jähriger deutſcher Junge   14jähriger Judenjunge   13jähriger Judenjunge

13jähriges deutſches Mädchen   8jähriges deutſches Mädchen   8jähriges Judenmädchen   14jähriges Judenmädchen

7jähriger deutſcher Junge   7jähriger Judenjunge

Aus dem Geſicht ſpricht die Seele der Raſſe

Left: This textbook prepared under the direction of the Nazis supposedly demonstrates the visible differences between Aryan children (on the left) and Jewish children (on the right).

Below: A Jewish girl smiles as she has her photograph taken.

A Letter from Adolf Hitler to Adolf Gemlich, September 16, 1919

There is evidence that Hitler's anti-Semitism was already firmly entrenched in 1919. While he was still in the army he was directed by the Press and Propaganda Office to report on the feelings of German soldiers toward the Jews. This is an extract from the report he sent to his immediate superior, Adolf Gemlich:

Anti-Semitism as a political movement should not and cannot be determined by emotional factors, but rather as a realization of the facts. And these facts are:

First Jewry is clearly a racial and not a religious group . . . . All that which is for men a source of higher life—be it religion, socialism, or democracy—is for the Jew merely a means to an end, namely, the satisfaction of his lust for power and money. His actions will result in a racial tuberculosis of peoples.

Hence it follows: Anti-Semitism based on purely emotional grounds will find its ultimate expression in the form of pogroms (which are capricious and thus not truly effective). Rational Anti-Semitism, however, must pursue a systematic, legal campaign against the Jews, by the revocation of the special privileges they enjoy in contrast to the other foreigners living among us. But the final objective must be the complete removal of the Jews.

(Quoted in Lucy S. Dawidowicz, *The War Against the Jews*)

Some Early Views of Hitler

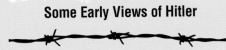

Konrad Heiden, a biologist who agreed with many of Hitler's racist views, described him like this in 1923:

Face and head: bad race, mongrel. Low receding forehead, ugly nose, broad cheekbones, small eyes, dark hair; facial expression, not of a man commanding with full self control, but betraying insane excitement. Finally an expression of blissful egotism…

Friedrich P. Reck-Malleczewen, in his book *Diary of a Man in Despair*, commented on an incident in which he saw Hitler alone in a restaurant:

If I had an inkling of the role this piece of filth was to play and of the years of suffering he was to make us endure, I would have done it [shot Hitler] without a second thought. But I took him for a character out of a comic strip and did not shoot.

(Quoted in Lucy S. Dawidowicz, *The War Against the Jews*)

Right: This carefully posed studio shot of Hitler shows an apparently even-tempered, calm, and thoughtful man. It contrasts sharply with the description by Konrad Heiden (left) and gives no hint of the hatred he and his party unleashed.

Some excerpts from *Mein Kampf*

Badly written, repetitive, and contradictory, Hitler's autobiography gives us some insight into his madness, egotism, and later actions. Here are a few examples of his many anti-Semitic outbursts in the book:

• The cleanliness of this people, moral and otherwise, I must say, is a point in itself. By their very exterior you could tell that these were no lovers of water, and, to your distress, you often knew it with your eyes shut…
• Was there any form of filth or profligacy, particularly in cultural life, without at least one Jew involved in it?…
• If you cut, even cautiously, into such an abscess, you found, like a maggot in a rotting body, often dazzled by the sudden light—a kike!…
• If, with the help of the Marxist creed, the Jew is victorious over the other peoples of this world, his crown will be the funeral wreath of humanity and this planet will, as it did thousands of years ago, move through the ether devoid of men…
• Hence today I believe that I am acting in accordance with the will of the Almighty Creator: *by defending myself against the Jew, I am fighting for the work of the Lord*…

(Quoted in F. Bradley Smith, *Adolf Hitler, His Family, Childhood and Youth*)

PAVING THE WAY FOR THE HOLOCAUST

IN 1933 Germany was still subject to the Treaty of Versailles, disarmed and economically fragile, so Hitler had to proceed carefully. A new Reichstag, elected in March, passed a law giving Hitler dictatorial powers. On the death of President Hindenburg in August 1934 Hitler became the *Führer* (leader) of the Third Reich. Emergency laws were quickly passed allowing for imprisonment without trial and state seizure of all communist property.

Some preliminary anti-Jewish measures were passed almost as soon as Hitler became chancellor. On April 1, 1933, a one-day boycott of all Jewish businesses was organized. Hitler had hoped to make it longer, but threats by other nations of a boycott of German goods made him back down.

Also in April 1933, a government decree ordered that all non-Aryan civil servants be dismissed from their posts. Jewish teachers were fired from universities, lawyers and judges from their posts, actors forbidden to perform, and musicians to play in concerts.

Below: An elderly Jewish man is stopped and tormented by Nazis in Berlin in 1934.

Alongside these formal attacks on the Jews, individual "actions" were carried out by the SA, or stormtroopers, the brownshirted Nazi paramilitary group. These actions involved beatings and, very occasionally, murders of individual Jews, as well as looting and burning synagogues. In April the Gestapo was established. This secret police force had the power to arrest and imprison

anyone without reference to any other state body, such as the court system.

In May a mass book burning was organized by Joseph Goebbels, the minister for propaganda. The books burned included anything written or published by Jews or other groups disliked by the Nazis. One famous German Jewish poet was Heinrich Heine, whose works also found their place on the bonfires. He had once written the prophetic line: "Those who begin by burning books end by burning people."

Siegbert Kinderman

Before Hitler came to power, those who attacked Jews were sometimes prosecuted. One such case was that of a baker's assistant from Berlin, Siegbert Kinderman. He had been attacked in the street by Nazis. They were arrested and convicted of assault. On March 18, 1933, the same men found Kinderman, took him to a SA barracks in Berlin, and beat him to death. His body was thrown out of a window. Witnesses noticed that a swastika had been cut into his chest.

Top: Heinrich Heine was a poet, essayist, and philosopher. He was born into a German Jewish family in 1797 but decided to convert to Christianity in 1825.

Above: Onlookers give the Nazi salute as books are burned in a huge bonfire in Berlin University Square, May 1933.

How Did Ordinary Germans React?

Historians differ as to how much support Nazi anti-Semitism had among "ordinary" Germans. Nazis organized the boycotts, led the physical attacks, and arrested Jews at random. But few people spoke out in opposition. Many benefited economically. Jews who wanted to leave Germany were forced to sell businesses and property to non-Jews at well below their real value. Other Germans took the place of Jews who lost their jobs.

Propaganda tried to convince Germans that the Jews were their enemies. Anti-Semitic newspapers such as *Der Stürmer* printed false stories like the one that appeared in 1934, under the headline "Jewish Murder Plot Against Non-Jewish Humanity is Uncovered," about ritual murder of Christian children. School textbooks contained grotesque cartoons of Jews. No doubt many people were influenced by such propaganda. Those who disagreed with the Nazis feared they would be arrested and punished. Even so, some Germans actively opposed the Nazis and even helped Jews—by hiding them, for example, once deportation to the camps began.

Left: In this propaganda from a German children's book, published in 1936, a well-off German couple is first seen consulting a Jewish lawyer. In the second picture the Germans have been reduced to poverty, while the fat, wealthy lawyer sits smoking a cigar.

Hitler's Views on Racial Purity

This extract is from a speech Hitler made at a 1929 Nazi party rally at Nuremberg:

As a result of our modern sentimental humanitarianism we are trying to maintain the weak at the expense of the healthy. It goes so far that a sense of charity which calls itself socially responsible is concerned to ensure that even cretins are able to procreate while more healthy people refrain from doing so... degenerates are raised artificially and with difficulty. In this way we are gradually breeding the weak and killing off the strong.

(Quoted in Alan Farmer, *Access to History in Depth: Anti-Semitism and the Holocaust*)

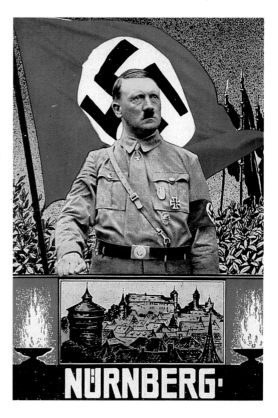

Above: Hitler looking stern at the Nuremberg party rally in 1929. He practiced his poses in front of a mirror in order to appear suitably authoritative.

The First Blows

The first organized blows against those considered the enemies of the state were not specifically against Jews. In March 1933 a concentration camp was established at Dachau, outside Munich, to hold 5,000 prisoners. Its opening was quickly followed by several more. The camps were soon filled with people taken into "protective custody"—Gypsies, habitual criminals, homosexuals, and some Jews. The inmates were forced into slave labor, and many of them died.

Although some of these first prisoners were Jews, they were imprisoned for their political opposition rather than their ethnic origin. At the same time official racial purification began with the passage of the Law for the Prevention of Offspring with Hereditary Diseases in July 1933. This allowed the forced sterilization of people who suffered from "feeble-mindedness," schizophrenia, epilepsy, blindness and deafness, deformities, and even alcoholism.

The Nuremberg Laws

In 1934 the attacks on Jews lessened and no new discriminatory laws were passed. In June, Hitler had 200 stormtroopers murdered in what became known as "the Night of the Long Knives." Led by Ernst Röhm, who was among those killed, the SA had become a potential threat to Hitler's power.

In May 1935 the Defense Law made non-Aryans ineligible for military service. Many Jews saw this as the final blow to their right to be German. The suicide rate among Jewish ex-soldiers rose to unprecedented levels in the months after this legislation was passed.

In September, the Nuremberg Laws were passed: Jews were denied their citizenship, and marriage and sexual relations between Jews and Germans were forbidden.

Jews were now defined as anyone with three or more Jewish grandparents, anyone with two Jewish grandparents who attended the synagogue, anyone who married a Jew after the enactment of the law, and any offspring of a mixed marriage born after the law was passed. This extended the number of people who could be treated as Jews to Christians whose parents or grandparents were Jews. Jews were forbidden to employ Aryan women under 45 as domestic help. Jews were designated

Above: A stormtrooper stands guard outside a Jewish shop during the boycott of 1933.

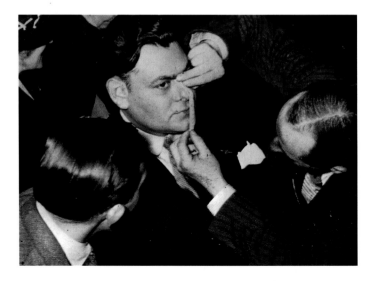

Left: Anyone suspected of having Jewish blood could expect to undergo tests such as this. This man's nose is being measured to see if he is Jewish

"subjects" but not citizens of Germany. Effectively, the Nuremberg laws left Jews without legal protection, and they were subject to any persecution that the Nazis chose to perpetrate.

This was followed in 1936 by a series of economic measures against those Jews who were still managing to run businesses in Germany. All businesses had to be "Aryanized"—this meant that Jewish assets were "transferred" into the hands of Nazi Party members, with tiny amounts paid in compensation.

Above: All Germans had to carry identification cards that could be checked at any time. Here, two civilian policemen stop a pedestrian and demand to see his identification papers.

Mischling

In Nazi Germany one's degree of Jewishness was vitally important. The Nuremberg Laws defined *mischling* (the word means "mixed") as half Jews and quarter Jews. Half-Jews were considered Jewish and were dismissed from government posts and subject to all the anti-Semitic laws. Quarter-Jews were sometimes considered Aryan and were allowed to attend schools, keep their jobs, and take part in the economic and social life of Germany. Some cases became very complex, and the German Ministry of the Interior's guidelines included some ludicrous examples. For instance, a fully Aryan woman who had married a Jew and practiced Judaism, and who was then widowed and married an Aryan, would apparently produce a Jewish child from the Aryan marriage. According to the Ministry, her grandchildren would be half Jewish.

Jewish Options

1. Emigration

Emigration was difficult. Other countries were reluctant to take in tens of thousands of impoverished refugees. Anti-Semitism existed elsewhere as well. Palestine was the obvious choice for many Jews, but Britain restricted the number of entry visas, fearing problems with the Arabs. Even the Zionist Jewish Agency for the resettlement of German Jews mainly sought young people with a trade or those able to bring some money from Germany. In general, young Jews found it easier to emigrate than did older Jews. Every year the Jewish population in Germany grew older as the young emigrated. By 1938, 150,000 Jews had left.

Opposite top: Polish refugees arrive in the safety of London in the summer of 1939.

2. Resistance

There were few opportunities to fight the German measures; when Jews did oppose them there were devastating consequences. One Jew who attempted to protest the 1938 expulsion of his parents from Germany was Hirschel Grynszpan. He went into the German Embassy in Paris, where he was a student, and shot a German official. The Nazis used the event to provoke a 24-hour pogrom all over Germany and Austria that later became known as *Kristallnacht* ("Night of the Broken Glass"). As well as convincing many Jews to leave Germany, *Kristallnacht* showed the Nazis that they could carry out such atrocities with impunity. It was an important milestone on the path toward the Holocaust.

3. Wait and Hope

Many Jewish families had lived in Germany since the 16th century or earlier. They considered themselves German. For 50 years they had enjoyed some degree of tolerance. They hoped that the persecution would soon end and Hitler would be deposed. Many Jews, especially the older ones who had invested their whole lives in the country, stayed in Germany hoping to ride out the storm. *Kristallnacht* changed all this.

Above: Passports of Jews were stamped with "J" to denote their religion, and they were forced to take the middle name "Sara" (for a woman) and "Israel" (for a man).

An Account of *Kristallnacht* by David Buffum, American Consul in Leipzig

At 3 am on November 10, 1938 was unleashed a barrage of Nazi ferocity as had no equal in Germany or very likely anywhere in the world since savagery began. Jewish buildings were smashed into and contents demolished or looted....

Having demolished buildings and hurled most of the moveable effects into the streets, the insatiably sadistic perpetrators threw many of the trembling inmates into a small stream...commanding horrified spectators to spit at them, defile them with mud and jeer at their plight.... These tactics were carried out the entire morning of the 10th November without police intervention and they were applied to men, women and children.

(Quoted in Alan Farmer, *Access to History in Depth: Anti-Semitism and the Holocaust*)

Above: The morning after Kristallnacht—a *Jewish store in Berlin has had its windows smashed.*

The Net Tightens

Less than a month before *Kristallnacht*, leaders of several European countries met at a conference at Evian in France to discuss the growing problem of Jewish refugees from Germany. Instead of condemning Germany or making emigration easier for refugees, the conference agreed not to interfere in internal German affairs. Of the 32 countries that participated, only Holland and Denmark agreed to increase the number of refugees they would take in.

By reassuring the Nazis that they could carry on as they wished with no outside interference, nations at the conference did great harm to German Jews. The Nazis were still encouraging Jews to emigrate, but other countries' reluctance to receive the refugees may have made them realize that since they would never be able to force all the Jews from Germany, a more radical solution to the "Jewish problem" would have to be found.

The refugee situation had already grown far worse within Germany's borders since its annexation of Austria in March 1938. Some 180,000 Austrian Jews became new subjects of the Nazis. Unlike the German Jews, who had gradually found

Left: Prime Minister Neville Chamberlain of Great Britain returned home from Germany in September 1938 promising "peace in our time." He had just agreed to let Germany take over the Sudetenland.

Left: The Sudetenland, which Germany seized in September 1938, extended the length of Czechoslovakia's borders with Germany and Austria.

themselves in this situation, the Austrian Jews became non-citizens overnight, had their property confiscated, and were actively encouraged to leave. When World War II broke out in 1939, 110,000 Jews had left Austria, mainly for neighboring countries, but their refuge was temporary.

The situation for the rest of Europe's Jews was growing worse. As Poland, Hungary, and other states realized that foreign powers were not going to intervene on behalf of the Jews, pogroms broke out in those countries. Hungary introduced its own set of anti-Jewish laws. Jews who had been driven out of Germany and into Poland were unwelcome there. Many were driven to the borders, had their property confiscated, and were left penniless. Some even tried to return to Germany and were shot.

In September 1938 Hitler demanded that the Sudetenland be ceded (handed over) to Germany. Unwilling to go to war, Great Britain and France agreed that Hitler should be given the Sudetenland, arguing that in doing so they had achieved "peace in our time." Meanwhile, even more Jews came under the power of the Nazis, and Hitler received an even stronger message that no one was prepared to stand up to him.

Hitler Speaks About the Jews at Konigsberg, before the Evian conference

I can only hope and expect that the other world, which has such deep sympathy for these criminals, will at least be generous enough to convert this sympathy into practical aid. We, on our part, are ready to put all these criminals at the disposal of these countries, for all I care, even on luxury ships.

(Quoted in Ronnie S. Landau, *The Nazi Holocaust*)

Above: Hitler with Admiral Miklos Horthy (center), Hungary's leader, in August 1938.

Nazi Anti-Jewish Policy on the Eve of World War II

Nazi leaders wanted the Jews to leave Germany as quickly as possible, but they also wanted to take all their money and property, which made them unattractive to the countries they applied to. At this stage there was no plan to exterminate all the Jews.

An important aspect of Nazi policy was the desire for *Lebensraum*—living space—for Germany's growing population. Hitler believed the countries east of Germany could provide such living space. He had already taken Austria and the Sudetenland in 1938, and Great Britain and France had done nothing. Now he set his sights on Poland and the Soviet Union, where he believed only "inferior [Slav] races" lived. Those countries were also home to millions of Jews.

The Nazis had hoped that the waves of Jewish refugees would trigger pogroms in the countries they fled to. In certain cases this did indeed occur, but pogroms—as Hitler had already pointed out—could not be relied upon.

The Nazis devised other plans. For instance, Lublin in Poland was to become a Jewish compound, but this came to nothing. Another plan, which was being discussed as late as 1940, involved resettling all the Jews on the island of Madagascar, off the east coast of Africa. It was assumed by the Nazi leadership that most of the Jews in these compounds would start to die of starvation and hardship fairly quickly.

German Foreign Ministry Memorandum on "The Jewish Question," January 25, 1939

The ultimate aim of Germany's policy is the emigration of all Jews living in German territory...

Germany has an important interest in seeing the splintering of Jewry...the influx of Jews arouses the resistance of the native population in all parts of the world and thus provides the best propaganda for Germany's policy toward the Jews.

(Quoted in Yitzhak Arad, Yisrael Gutman, and Abraham Margaliot (eds), *Documents on the Holocaust*)

Above: Joachim von Ribbentrop was Germany's foreign minister from 1938 to 1945.

HOW THE HOLOCAUST HAPPENED

THE EARLY years of Nazi rule had a positive effect on Germany's economy. Unemployment fell sharply. Ignoring the Treaty of Versailles, which had restricted German arms manufacture and the size of its armed forces, the Nazis built a war economy with massive rearmament. Germany added much new territory. All trade unions and political parties other than the Nazis were outlawed. Universal military service was introduced. Having rearmed and prepared Germany for war, Hitler's only anxiety was that Great Britain or France might intervene.

Below left: Victims of the German invasion, these Polish children fled from Warsaw with their parents into territory that had been seized by the Soviet Union. They were then returned to Poland, forced back to Soviet Russia, and finally sent back once again to Warsaw.

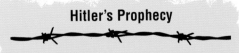

Hitler's Prophecy

In a speech on January 30, 1939, Hitler issued a warning to the world that if anything bad happened to Germany the Jews would suffer:

Today I will once more be a prophet: if the international Jewish financiers in and outside Europe should succeed in plunging the nations once more into a world war, then the result will not be the Bolshevization of the earth and thus the victory of Jewry but the annihilation of the Jewish race in Europe.

(Quoted in Lucy S. Dawidowicz, *The War Against the Jews*)

The Invasion of Poland

Not satisfied with just the Sudetenland, Germany invaded Czechoslovakia in March 1939, and thousands more Jews came under Nazi control. After this latest outrage both Great Britain and France promised Poland protection. Even so, Hitler was surprised when Great Britain and France declared war in September 1939 following the invasion of Poland. Of the 3,300,000 Jews living in Poland, many were able to flee eastward into the Soviet Union. But two million were trapped in Nazi-held Poland.

Above: German soldiers march through the Austrian border town of Kufstein in 1938. The crowd cheers them on and waves Nazi flags.

The "Jewish Question" in the Occupied Territory of Poland

In 1939 Reinhard Heydrich, head of the Nazi security police, was given responsibility for transporting all the Jews in occupied Poland by railroad to closed areas, from where they would easily be moved on to their final destination. On September 20 he issued these instructions:

I refer to the conference held in Berlin today and again point out that planned total measures (i.e., the final aim) are to be kept strictly secret.
A distinction must be made between:

1. The final aim (which will require extended periods of time) and
2. the stages leading to the fulfillment of this final aim…

For the time being the final prerequisite for the final aim is the concentration of the Jews from the countryside into the larger cities. This is to be carried out speedily . . . . In this connection it should be borne in mind that only cities which are railroad junctions, or at least located on railroad lines, should be selected as concentration points.

(Quoted in Ronnie S. Landau, *Studying the Holocaust*)

Above: Heinrich Himmler (third from left) was second only to Hitler in power in Nazi Germany. Reinhard Heydrich (third from right) was the head of the security police. The two were instrumental in planning the Final Solution.

The Consequences for the Jews

As German troops made their way across Poland, the majority of Jews were forced into slave labor, and thousands were slaughtered. Many were driven out of their homes and into Russian-held territory.

A special task force, the *Einsatzgruppen*, was created to carry out Heydrich's orders of rounding up Jews from the countryside and herding them into closed ghettos in the cities. Councils of Jewish elders were set up to take a census of the Jews in their areas. Jews from the Sudetenland and Czechoslovakia were forcibly shipped to Poland to live in the Polish ghettos, many of them dying en route. Labor camps were set up all over Poland, particularly along the Soviet border, where Jews were put to labor digging trenches and building fortifications. Near Gdansk (Danzig) a special camp was used to kill mentally disabled people from Poland and Germany. At first men were snatched off the streets and sent to the labor camps, but later the Jewish Councils in each city were given the job of providing labor brigades.

Above: Inmates of Dachau concentration camp being used as beasts of burden.

Within the ghettos people began to die of starvation. By October 1940 most of the ghettos were sealed. Sanitation was poor, and starvation rations were given to people who were forced into grueling labor each day. There was a danger that epidemics might spread from the ghettos into the rest of the cities. All over Poland the numbers of people trapped in the ghettos rose daily, even with the high death rate from disease, starvation, and suicide. All emigration from Poland was banned—on the grounds that any Jews who escaped might organize a war of revenge against Germany. Then, in June 1941, Germany broke its peace treaty with the Soviet Union and invaded.

An Eyewitness Account of the Warsaw Ghetto by Stanislav Rozykzi

On the streets children are crying in vain, children who are dying of hunger. They howl, beg, sing, moan, shiver with cold, without underwear, without clothing, without shoes, in rags, sacks, flannel which are bound in strips around the emaciated skeletons, children swollen with hunger, disfigured, half conscious, already completely grown up at the age of five, gloomy and weary of life.

There are not only children. Young and old people, men and women, bourgeois and proletarian, intelligentsia and business people are all being declassed and degraded. They beg for one month, for two months, for three months—but they all go downhill and die in the streets . . . .

(Quoted in Ronnie S. Landau, *The Nazi Holocaust*)

Left: As adults died or were arrested, more and more children were left abandoned in the Warsaw ghetto. Some survived by dealing on the black market, running errands, or finding some kind of work. Others died on the streets or were sent to the camps themselves.

The "Jewish Question"

At this stage, the Nazis had not yet decided on their answer to the "Jewish Question." Policy towards the Jews varied enormously from one country to another. In Germany Jews could still emigrate if they could find a country to take them, while in Poland Jews from all over German-occupied territory were trapped in ghettos, starving to death and forced to work for the German war effort. German troops shot, tortured, and maimed Jews at the slightest excuse, and Jewish people were robbed of all their possessions. But, as yet, the massacres were relatively small in scale and not a specific policy.

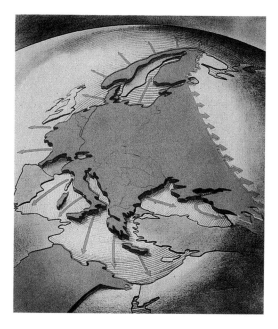

Above: This illustration from a French magazine, published in 1942, shows the German advance across Europe and North Africa.

By June 1940 Germany had invaded and occupied Denmark, Norway, Belgium, France, and Holland, bringing another 550,000 Jews (as well as refugees who had already fled from Germany) under Nazi control. The numbers of Jews the Germans planned to remove from German-controlled lands grew daily. The invasion of the Soviet Union brought several million more Jews under German occupation.

Did the Nazis Plan the Holocaust?

Historians are divided about the Nazis' ultimate plan. Some believe that the Nazis always intended to carry out genocide, and that by 1941 events had made this possible. They refer to some of the statements made by Hitler and other Nazis prior to this time to prove that they always had murderous intentions. Others believe that the Nazis initially wanted to force all Jews to emigrate or resettle in special compounds and that the idea of eliminating all Europe's Jews only came to seem the most practical "solution" as the war progressed.

Numbers of Jews in Nazi-occupied Europe in 1941

Poland	3,300,000
Czechoslovakia	315,000
France	300,000
Germany	210,000
Holland	150,000
Belgium	90,000
Austria	60,000
Yugoslavia (invaded 1941)	75,000
Greece (invaded 1941)	75,000
Others	20,000

Below: The devastation of war. A town in the Ukraine is wiped out by the German advance. Behind these troops came the Einsatzgruppen, eliminating communist officials and Jews.

Barbarossa and Genocide

On June 22, 1941, German troops invaded the Soviet Union, an operation code-named Barbarossa. Before they invaded, Hitler told his generals that they should be merciless to the Slavs and doubly merciless to Slav communists. The *Einsatzgruppen* (special SS units) would follow the army, and in every conquered area they were to shoot all communist officials. However the real order was to exterminate all Soviet Jews. Once the invasion got under way, the *Einsatzgruppen* carried out mass murders of more than a million Jews over a period of 18 months in the Baltic states and the eastern territories of the Soviet Union.

The First Gas Chambers

From January 1940 to August 1941, the Nazis carried out a euthanasia program, in which 90,000 elderly, handicapped, "socially defective," and mentally disturbed Germans were put to death. The official program stopped

An *Einsatzgruppen* action, observed by Herman Gräbe, a German builder

The bodies were lying so tightly packed together that only their heads showed.... Some were still moving . . . . The ditch was already three-quarters full. I estimate that it held about a thousand bodies. I turned my eyes toward the man doing the shooting. He was an SS man; he sat, legs swinging, on the edge of the ditch. He had an automatic rifle resting on his knees and he was smoking a cigarette. The people, completely naked, climbed down steps which had been cut into the clay wall of the ditch, stumbled over the heads of those lying there and stopped at the spot indicated by the SS man. They lay down on top of the dead and wounded; some stroked those still living and spoke quietly to them. Then I heard a series of rifle shots. I looked into the ditch and saw the bodies contorting or, the heads already inert, sinking on the corpses beneath.

(Quoted in Ronnie S. Landau, *The Nazi Holocaust*)

in September for fear of public outcry, but the psychiatric patients continued to be killed in the hospitals and later in the death camps. Gas chambers were one method of murder. In that same autumn some Soviet prisoners of war were murdered using Zyklon B gas. In the summer Heinrich Himmler had ordered the construction of a death camp at Auschwitz, incorporating gas chambers disguised as showers and crematoriums for disposing of the bodies.

Above: Crematorium ovens used to destroy the bodies of the victims. Sometimes, if the victims were very thin, two or three bodies could be burned at a time.

The Beginnings of Mass Murder

These events showed the Nazi regime that they could get ordinary citizens—doctors and nurses at six killing centers in Germany and members of *Einsatzgruppen* units in Poland, the Baltic states, and the easternmost territories of the Soviet Union—to murder innocent people. The experiments with Zyklon B on prisoners at Auschwitz, and the use of gas vans to kill Jews from the Lodz ghetto provided the Nazis with useful information on the most effective means of destruction.

In October 1941 the first mass transports of Jews began. Jews from Austria, Germany, and Czechoslovakia were taken to the cities of Riga, Minsk, and Kaunas and were shot or herded into ghettos. In November 1941 five transports of Jews were murdered on arrival at Kaunas. Also in November, 14,000 Jews in Riga were murdered, along with 1,000 more from Berlin.

In January 1942 a conference was held at Wannsee in Berlin to discuss the "Final Solution." It was chaired by Reinhard Heydrich, but the decisions had already been made at the highest levels of Nazi authority. Conference members learned that all remaining Jews were to be taken from every country in occupied Europe to work camps. Survivors of the forced labor would be put to death.

Opposite: How Europe's Jews were marked out for death at the Wannsee conference. The boxed totals show the Nazi's estimates of the number of Jews to be transported from each country.

ZYGMUNT BENSZ

Left: Jews on their way to the Lodz ghetto, March 1940. They were allowed to take some basic furniture and possessions with them. When they left Lodz, bound for the death camps, they could carry only one bag and some food for the journey.

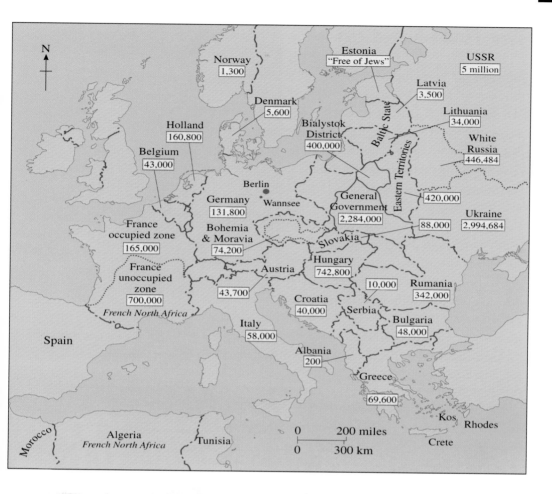

Minutes of the Wannsee Conference

The Jews are to be utilized for work in the East in an *expedient manner in the course of the final solution. In large columns, with the sexes* separated, Jews capable of work will be moved into those areas as they build roads, during which a large proportion will no doubt drop out through natural reduction. *The remnant that eventually remains will require* suitable treatment; *because it will without* doubt represent the most physically resistant part, it consists of a natural selection that could, *on its release, become the germ cell of*

a new Jewish revival (*witness the experience of* history). Europe is to be combed through from *West to East in the course of the practical* implementation of the final solution...

The evacuated Jews will be first taken group by group to so-called transit ghettos, in order to be transported further east . . . .

Italics have been added to highlight phrases used instead of "slave labor," "death," and "extermination."

(Quoted in Ronnie S. Landau, *Studying the Holocaust*)

The Final Solution

Between 1941 and Germany's surrender in 1945, it is estimated that about 6.2 million Jews died. More than two million people were gunned down beside mass graves, and over three million were murdered in specially built Polish death camps. Hundreds of thousands were worked or starved to death in labor camps and ghettos or died in cattle cars en route to the death camps or on the death marches away from the liberating Soviet army.

Most Jews did not actively resist their murderers, partly because the Germans went to great lengths to prevent them from realizing what was happening—right up to the doors of the gas chambers. Some believe that the actions of Jewish leaders actually increased the death toll. One political theorist, Hannah Arendt, controversially claimed that: "…if the Jewish people had been disorganized and leaderless there would have been chaos and plenty of misery but the total number of dead would hardly have been six million."

Below: Starving Jewish children being transported from the Warsaw ghetto to Auschwitz

Letter from One of the *Einsatzkommandos*

For we must finish matters once and for all and finally settle accounts with war criminals in order to create a better and eternal Germany for our heirs . . . . There are three or four operations a week, sometimes Gypsies, another time Jews, partisans and all sorts of trash... when an action requires immediate atonement... and justice takes its course. If the official judicial system were operating it would be impossible to exterminate a whole family when only the father is guilty....

I am grateful for having been allowed to see this bastard race close up.... Syphilitics, cripples, idiots were typical of them... they were materialists to the end. They were saying things like "We are skilled workers, you are not going to kill us." They were not men but monkeys in human form.

Ah well, there is only a small percentage of the 24,000 Jews of Kamentz-Podolsk left. The Yids in the surrounding area are also clients of ours. We are ruthlessly making a clean sweep with a clear conscience and then... the waves close over, the world has peace.

(Quoted in J. Noakes and G. Pridham (eds) *Nazism 1919–1945*)

The Jewish Councils drew up lists of deportees, policed the ghettos, kept order for the Nazis, and even drove the deportees onto the trains. They arranged social and cultural activities in the ghettos, trying to create an atmosphere of normality in an abnormal situation. But many members of the Jewish Councils knew nothing about the death camps. Those who did know felt they had no choice—if they had not cooperated, they and their families would have been killed. Others believed that if they kept the ghettos producing, at least some Jews would be saved because they were necessary to the war effort.

Right: Hannah Arendt was a Jewish philosopher whose family escaped Germany in 1940. She reported on the 1961 trial of Adolf Eichmann, who organized the delivery of millions of Jews to the gas chambers.

EXPLAINING THE HOLOCAUST

IN THE preceding chapters we have seen how Germany moved toward the Final Solution, driven by racial prejudice, economic and military collapse after World War I, the need for a scapegoat, and the reluctance of other nations to act. It seems that the Nazis initially wanted to get rid of the Jews by means of forced emigration and resettlement. The idea of physically exterminating them only gradually emerged as the war progressed and Germany occupied territory to the east—land that Hitler wanted as living space and that was home to millions of Jews.

The genocide that took place in the following years was one of the worst atrocities in human history. In the last days of the war, facing certain defeat, the Nazis continued to kill Jews out of continued anti-Semitic hatred, a sense of duty to the government, frustrated vengeance, and the desire to ensure that no survivors would be left to testify about the Holocaust.

Below: French Jews approach the freight cars that will take them to the death camps. They were told to take luggage with them, but this was only to reassure them. When they arrived in Poland most of these people would have been gassed immediately and their possessions searched for valuables to be sent back to Germany.

The Allies must also bear some responsibility for the success of the Holocaust. In 1939, when the Soviet Union divided Poland with Germany, Great Britain, France, and the United States were unable or unwilling to act. It is known now that the U.S. government had evidence of the gas chambers as early as 1942, and Great Britain continued to make it impossible for escapees to enter Palestine throughout the war. Eastern European countries gladly rounded up Jews and sent them to the death camps, while occupied France introduced anti-Semitic laws without even being forced to. Even in the Channel Islands, British policemen helped transport Jews to the camps.

Below: Winston Churchill, prime minister of Great Britain, gives his famous victory salute.

British Anti-Semitism

In the *Illustrated Sunday Herald* of February 8, 1920, Winston Churchill, who would lead Great Britain in World War II, once wrote about a "worldwide Jewish conspiracy":

This movement [meaning communism] among the Jews is not new. From the days of ... Karl Marx and down to Trotsky (Russia), Bela Kun (Hungary), Rosa Luxemburg (Germany) and Emma Goldman (United States) this worldwide Jewish conspiracy for the overthrow of civilization and for the reconstitution of society on the basis of an arrested development, of envious malevolence, and impossible equality has been steadily growing.

The Nature of Nazism

The machinery of the Nazi state successfully created an atmosphere where citizens believed that Jews were the enemy and somehow less than human. It was forbidden to call the victims "people" or refer to their bodies as "corpses." They were to be called "the load," "merchandise," "pieces," or "sticks."

Historians disagree about the role of ordinary Germans. Some believe that their apathy was due to years of relying on authoritarian government to decide what was best for them. Others believe that German society was guilty because it had allowed the Nazis into power. Others argue that most Germans were also prisoners of the regime, unable to pose any meaningful opposition. Many Jews did not believe the rumors that filtered back to the ghettos about the gassings, so it is possible that the majority of Germans, involved in food shortages and bombing raids, with their families fighting on many fronts, also knew little about the ultimate fate of the Jews. One historian, Ian Kershaw, has said, "The road to Auschwitz was built by hate but paved with indifference."

Below: At center is Rudolf Höss, the first commandant of Auschwitz. In his memoirs, written while awaiting trial for war crimes, he expressed pride in his actions. He was convicted and executed outside Auschwitz in 1947.

Above: The railroad tracks leading to Auschwitz

From the Memoirs of Rudolf Höss, Commandant of Auschwitz

...it was ... already taken for granted that the Jews were to blame for everything... It was not just newspapers like the Stürmer but it was everything we ever heard. Even our military and ideological training took for granted that we had to protect Germany from the Jews . . . . It only started to occur to me after the collapse that maybe it was not quite all right, after I heard what everyone was saying . . . .

Now I wonder if Himmler really believed all that himself or just gave me an excuse to justify what he wanted me to do. But anyway, that really didn't matter. We were all so trained to obey orders without even thinking that the thought of disobeying an order would simply never have occurred to anybody and somebody else would have done just as well if I hadn't . . . .

You can be sure that it wasn't always a pleasure to see those mountains of corpses or smell the continual burning. But Himmler had ordered it and had explained the necessity and I really never gave much thought to whether it was wrong. It just seemed a necessity.

(Quoted in Gustav Gilbert, *Nuremberg Diary*)

Was the Holocaust Unique?

Many people argue that the Holocaust was a unique event in world history. They would agree that other episodes of genocide have taken place, but they believe that the Holocaust stands alone and thereby deserves special attention. They argue, for example, for the adoption of Holocaust remembrance days and the inclusion of special Holocaust lessons and material in school curriculum. It is only by remembering, they believe, and by emphasizing the special horror of the Holocaust, that humanity can ensure that it will never happen again.

However, others argue that to emphasize the uniqueness of the Holocaust is to minimize and downplay the suffering of other peoples who have been targeted for genocide. In just the last decade, wholesale massacres of people singled out for their racial or ethnic background have occurred between Hutus and Tutsis in Rwanda and Burundi, in Africa, and between Serbs and Croats in

Below: Children who survived the massacres in Rwanda wait in a refugee camp for food.

the former Yugoslavia. These killings fit the United Nations' definition of genocide. Some people believe that by insisting that the Holocaust is special, it somehow makes it easier to overlook or ignore these other tragedies.

There is at least one way in which the Holocaust is unique: Never before had a government set in motion a specific policy intended to result ultimately in the death of every single person of a specific ethnic or religious background. One must hope that in this regard the Holocaust remains unique.

Below: These starving Muslim refugees were liberated from a Croat concentration camp in the former Yugoslavia in 1993. Most had lost 44 lb (20 kg) or more during their captivity.

I still do not understand why I did not throw myself upon the kapo who was beating my father before my very eyes. In Galicia, Jews dug their own graves and lined up, without any traces of panic, at the edge of the trench to await the machine-gun barrage. I do not understand their calm. And that woman, that mother, in the bunker somewhere in Poland, I do not understand her either, her companions smothered her child for fear its cries might betray their presence; that woman, that mother, having lived that scene of biblical intensity, did not go mad. I do not understand her; why and by what right, and in the name of what, did she not go mad?

I do not know why, but I forbid us to ask the question.

(From Elie Wiesel, *Legends of Our Time*)

DATE LIST

922 B.C.	Kingdom of Judah is established
A.D. 70	Kingdom of Judah falls to the Romans
11th/12th centuries	Massacres of Jews in the Rhineland
1215	European Jews forced to wear distinctive clothes
1290	Jews expelled from England
1306	Jews expelled from France
1648	Massacres of Jews in Poland and Ukraine
19th century	Jewish emancipation in Germany and other Western European states
1827	Russian Jewish boys forced to join Russian army
1881	Assassination of Czar triggers pogroms in Russia
1889	Birth of Hitler in Austria
1914–18	World War I; Jews fight in German, British, French, Italian armies
1919	Treaty of Versailles punishes Germany
1919	Pogroms in Eastern European states
1921	Hitler becomes leader of NSDAP, or Nazi Party
1923	Hitler's beer hall uprising; Hitler is imprisoned and writes *Mein Kampf*
1926	Hitler Youth and other minority groups formed
1933	Hitler becomes chancellor; concentration camps established for "enemies of the state"
1934	Nuremberg Laws deprive German Jews of their citizenship
1938	*Kristallnacht*—a wave of terror is unleashed on German Jews
1939	World War II begins when Poland is invaded; ghettos established in Polish cities
1940	Germany invades Denmark, Norway, France, Belgium, and Holland
1941	Operation Barbarossa, the invasion of the Soviet Union; *Einsatzgruppen* squads massacre Jews
late 1941	Death camp added to existing concentration camp at Auschwitz; euthanasia program in Germany
January 1942	Wannsee conference establishes means of transporting the Jews to their deaths
1941–45	The Final Solution is implemented throughout occupied Europe
1945	World War II ends

RESOURCES

FURTHER READING AND SOURCES

Bauer, Yehuda. *History of the Holocaust.* Danbury, CT: Franklin Watts, 1992.

Dawidowicz, Lucy. *The War Against the Jews.* New York: Penguin, 1990.

Frank, Anne. *The Diary of Anne Frank.* New York: Bantam, 1993.

Friedlander, Saul. *Nazi Germany and the Jews: The Years of Persecution 1933-1939.* New York: HarperCollins, 1998.

Gilbert, Martin. *The Holocaust.* New York: Henry Holt, 1987.

Grant, R. G. *The Holocaust: New Perspectives.* New York: Raintree Steck-Vaughn, 1998.

Gutman, Israel. *Resistance: The Warsaw Ghetto Uprising.* New York: Houghton-Mifflin, 1997.

Hilberg, Raul. *The Destruction of the European Jews.* Holmes and Meier, 1985.

Keneally, Thomas. *Schindler's List.* Touchstone, 1993.

Laquer, Walter (ed). *The Holocaust Encyclopedia.* New Haven, CT: Yale University Press, 2001.

Levi, Primo. *Survival in Auschwitz.* New York: Simon and Schuster, 1996.

Rohrlich, Ruby (ed.) *Resisting the Holocaust.* New York: Berg, 1998.

Wiesel, Elie. *Night.* New York: Bantam, 1982.

INTERNET SITES

Shoah Visual History Foundation
www.vhf.org
Photographs and stories by survivors.

United States Holocaust Memorial Museum
www.ushmn.org
Pictorial history of the Holocaust

Yad Veshem
www.yad-vashem.org
Official website for the Holocaust Martyrs' and Heroes' Remembrance Authority

FILMS

The following movies are available for rent as videos or DVDs:

Schindler's List. Directed by Steven Spielberg from the book by Thomas Keneally, this is the story of a German factory owner who saved more than 1,000 Jews.

Shoah. Directed by Claude Lanzmann, this is a nine-hour documentary consisting entirely of interviews with survivors of and participants in the Holocaust.

Life is Beautiful. Directed by and starring Roberto Benigni, this controversial, Academy Award-winning film tells the fictional tale of an Italian Jewish father who creates a kind of make-believe contest out of the Nazi occupation in order to shelter his son from the horrors of the Holocaust.

PLACES TO VISIT

United States Holocaust Memorial Museum
100 Raoul Wallenberg Place SW
Washington, D.C. 20024
Phone: (202) 488-0400
Website: www.ushm.org
Library: library@ushm.org
(202) 479-9717

GLOSSARY

Allies countries that fought in World War II against Germany, Japan, and their allies.

anti-Semitism prejudice against Jewish people.

appease to pacify, satisfy, or settle a dispute.

Aryan the Nazis used this term to mean a white-skinned person, not of Jewish, gypsy, or Slavic origin. They believed Aryans were members of a superior race that the Jews were trying to corrupt.

Baltic states the states of Estonia, Latvia, and Lithuania, which became part of the Soviet Union in 1940 and regained their independence in the early 1990s.

Barbarossa the code name for the German invasion of Russia, June 22, 1941.

Black Death a terrible disease that killed about a third of all the people in Europe in the Middle Ages; now known as bubonic plague.

Bolsheviks left wing party that seized power in Russia after the Russian Revolution.

bureaucracy a system or organization involving a lot of officials, paperwork, and regulations.

communism the theory that all property should be state-owned and that each person should be paid according to his or her needs.

concentration camps large-scale prison and work camps, where prisoners were often worked to death but not in the systematic manner of the death camps.

crematoriums places where corpses are disposed of by burning.

death camps also known as extermination camps, designed to systematically murder their inmates, mostly Jews. All the Nazi death camps were in Poland: Auschwitz, Belzec, Chelmno, Majdanek, Sobibor, and Treblinka. (Some were also labor/concentration camps.)

deportation the process of removing people from their homes and taking them to a death, labor, or concentration camp in the east.

Der Stürmer anti-Semitic weekly German newspaper.

Einsatzgruppen special units ordered to eliminate enemies of the state and mainly responsible for the mass killing of Jews and communists in occupied Poland and Russia.

emancipation equality with all members of a state and the freedom to take part in the political, economic, and cultural life of that state.

Enlightenment a European intellectual movement that reached its peak in the eighteenth century. Philosophers of the Enlightenment believed in social and scientific progress and were critical of religion and class structure.

extermination complete destruction of a race or species.

fascism a political movement, led by Benito Mussolini, that developed in Italy in the 1920s; a political system that aims to unite a country's people into a disciplined force under an all-powerful leader.

Final Solution from the Nazi term *Endlösung*. The phrase "Final Solution of the Jewish Question" was used when referring to the extermination of all European Jews.

genocide deliberate destruction of a racial, religious, political, or ethnic group.

Gestapo the German secret police during the rule of the Nazis.

ghettos the poorest districts in some European towns and cities, where Nazis forced Jews to live and from where they were transported to death camps.

Holocaust term used since World War II to refer to the murder of some six million Jews.

idolatry worshiping idols (images of gods).

kapos selected prisoners, put in charge of ordinary prisoners, who managed many of the daily routines of camp life.

Kristallnacht in English "Night of the Broken Glass." On November 9/10, 1938, in retaliation for the murder of a German diplomat in Paris, Jewish homes and businesses in Germany were attacked and Jews were injured, humiliated, and in some cases murdered.

labor camps camps using slave labor, mostly prisoners of war and Jews, to increase Germany's wartime production.

lebensraum in English "living space," land that Hitler wished to see colonized by Germans in eastern Europe.

mischling literally means "mixed."

Nazi Party (*Nationalsozialistische Deutsche Arbeiterpartei*) in English "National Socialist German Workers' Party." Led by Hitler, the Nazi Party governed Germany between 1933 and 1945.

Palestine the area formerly known as Judah, the ancient land of the Jews. In 1948 the Jewish state of Israel was created in Palestine.

pogrom an organized massacre of members of a particular section of society, used especially when referring to attacks on Jews in Russia.

Reichstag the German parliament.

SS (*Schutzstaffel*) in English "protection squads." Originally used as bodyguards to protect senior members of the Nazi Party, the SS developed into its most powerful organization and was responsible for controlling the concentration and death camps.

Stormtroopers known in Germany as the SA (*Sturmabteilung*), these shock troops were established in 1921; they kept order at Nazi meetings and beat up opponents.

swastika ancient Buddhist symbol that the Nazis adopted as their emblem.

Talmud a collection of ancient writings on Jewish religious law and tradition.

volksgemeinschaft the national community of Germany, united by their German blood and not divided by class, religion, or politics.

usury lending money at a high rate of interest.

USSR abbreviation for the Union of Soviet Socialist Republics, dominated by Russia, which broke up at the end of the 1980s.

Yiddish the language spoken by Jews in Europe. It was a mixture of German, Slavic, and Hebrew words and was written down using Hebrew characters.

Zionism Jewish nationalist movement that aimed to found a Jewish national homeland in Palestine.

INDEX